"狗狗忙碌的一天"的赞美
Praise for "Doggy's Busy Day

作为九个孩子的爷爷，一个年级较小的孩子坐在我的大腿上不断地恳求我讲一个故事。
由Jayne FLaagan发行的书"狗狗忙碌的一天"一举成名，不仅可以大声地读出来，而且还可以与她提出的问题进行互动。我希望所有的儿童书籍都可以使用类似的格式。还是一份很棒的礼物。五星！~ Mike Lewis

由Jayne Flaagan写的 "狗狗忙碌的一天"是一本非常吸引儿童的书籍，书中有许多她的可爱的哈士奇狗的照片。
每个页面嵌入的问题邀请了孩子参与并引发了他们以及陪伴阅读的大人们的思考，随着时间的推移可以扩展到更复杂的对话。更重要的是，该书的结构为带狗狗度过平常的一天，这样一来可以为读者提供一个并行支持结构。这些元素是早期学习成功的关键。尽情享受吧！~ Donna Kim-Brand

Jayne Flaagan 的书"狗狗忙碌的一天"是一个迷人的视觉享受，该书的特色为配有很多哈士奇狗Ella的照片。书里全是Ella的彩色照片并且摆着各种各样的姿势，这本书让孩子注意到了自己和小狗之间的相似之处。这本书一定会让任何孩子都爱不释手。~ Hiyaguha Cohen

Praise for "Doggy's Busy Day"

"As the grandfather of nine, I have a young child in my lap constantly begging for a story. Jayne FLaagan's book "Doggy's Busy Day" has been a hit, not only reading it aloud, but interacting with the questions she provides. I wish all children's books would use a similar format. A great gift, too. Five stars!" ~ Mike Lewis

"Doggy's Busy Day" by Jayne Flaagan is an appealing book for young children, supported by photos of her adorable husky dog. Don't let the simple format fool you into thinking this is a passive read. The questions embedded in each page invite engagement and consideration by the youngsters and their adult reading companions relevant to their own life, possibly extending into more complex conversations over time. What's more, the book is structured to take the doggie through a normal day, which can provide a parallel support structure for the reader. These elements are crucial in early learning success. Enjoy! ~ Donna Kim-Brand

Jayne Flaagan's book "Doggy's Busy Day" is a charming visual treat, featuring the photogenic husky, Ella. Filled with full-page color photos of Ella in numerous lovable poses, the book asks young readers to notice the similarities between the pup and themselves. This book is sure to be requested over and over by any child. ~ Hiyaguha Cohen

"狗狗忙碌的一天"对我的家人都做出了奉献，为了书中的照片，他们帮助鼓励Ella "做足了表演"。

"Doggy's Busy Day" is dedicated to my family, who helped encourage Ella to
"ham it up" for the pictures included in this book.

Jayne Flaagan有着30余年的幼儿教育经验和教育背景。她获得了很多快乐并且对这种类型的工作很满意。Flaagan在北达科塔州长大并在多年前搬到了明尼苏达州。她和他的丈夫以及那只名叫Ella的萌狗居住在一起。她还有三个成年子女。

Jayne Flaagan的网站为：www.ellathedoggy.com。
你可以在djflaagan@gra.midco.net阅读更多有关她的资料。

Jayne Flaagan has over 30 years of experience and education in Early Childhood Education. She receives much joy and satisfaction working in this genre. Flaagan grew up in North Dakota and made the big move to Minnesota many years ago.
She lives with her husband and a goofy dog named Ella. She has three grown children.

You can contact her at djflaagan@gra.midco.net

You can reach her at djflaagan@gra.midco.net

这是狗狗Ella。

她有两只眼睛。她有两只耳朵。

她有一只鼻子。她有一张嘴。

和你一样。

This is Ella the Doggy.
She has two eyes. She has two ears.
She has one nose. She has one mouth.
Just like you.

Ella有四条腿和一个尾巴。

你有几条腿呢？

你有小尾巴吗？

Ella has four legs and one tail.

How many legs do you have?

Do you have a tail?

当Ella早晨醒来的时候,她会伸个大懒腰!

当你伸懒腰的时候是什么感觉呢?

When Ella wakes up in the morning, she gives herself a very big stretch!

How does that feel when you stretch?

当Ella早晨醒来的时候会非常的饿，所以她开始准备早餐。

她是如此的饿，她正舔着嘴唇。

你吃饭的时候带着口水兜吗？

Ella is very hungry when she wakes up, so she gets ready for breakfast.

She is so hungry, she is licking her lips.

Do you wear a bib when you eat?

有时候Ella会坐起来要吃的东西。

她不会说"请"因为狗狗是不会说话的。

当你想要东西的时候你会说什么呢？

Sometimes Ella will sit up and ask for food.
She cannot say "please" because doggies cannot talk.
What do you say when you want something?

Ella是在一个白色的碗里吃早餐。

碗都被嚼坏了，
因为她的牙齿很锋利并且她喜欢玩那个碗。

Ella eats her breakfast from a white bowl.

The bowl is all chewed up because she has sharp teeth and she likes to play with it.

狗狗还喝很多的水。

Ella从一个蓝色的碗里喝水。

你是用什么来喝水的呢？

Doggies drink lots of water too.
Ella drinks from a blue bowl.
What do you use to drink water?

Ella现在要出去散步了。她非常的激动！

Ella is going on a walk now. She is very excited!

她喜欢到外面散步呼吸新鲜空气。

为了变得强壮你做什么运动呢？

She loves to walk outside in the fresh air.

What do you do to exercise so you can grow big and strong?

即使是外面非常的冷，Ella还是会出去散步。

你居住的地方会下雪吗？

Even when it is cold outside, Ella takes a walk.

Do you have snow where you live?

散步之后Ella有点累了，所以她来到太阳底下小睡一会。

你在哪儿休息呢？

After her walk Ella is tired, so she naps in the sun.

Where do you rest?

Ella现在有点不开心了。

她想找一个玩伴。

Ella is sad right now.
She wants someone to play with.

Ella现在很开心因为她看到了她的一个朋友！

当你不开心的时候你看上去是什么样的呢？

当你开心的时候看上去又是什么样的呢？

Now Ella is happy because she sees a friend!

What does your face look like when you are sad?

How does your face look when you are happy?

这是Ella，那是她还很小。

她正在和她的朋友Daisy玩耍。

你的朋友的名字叫什么呢？

This is Ella when she was smaller.

She is playing with her friend Daisy.

What are the names of your friends?

有时候Ella会和她的人类朋友去野餐。

你去野餐的时候都吃些什么呢？

Sometimes Ella has picnics with her people friends.

What do you eat when you go on a picnic?

看看谁在装傻了！

当你装傻的时候你会怎么做呢？

Look who is being silly!

What do you do when you act silly?

Ella也很喜欢玩游戏。

有时候她会玩一个名叫拔河比赛的游戏。

Ella likes to play games too.

Sometimes she plays a game called *Tug-Of-War*.

Ella正在玩另一个游戏。

她必须找到那只握着她的玩具的手。

你能帮她找到那个玩具吗？

Here is Ella playing another game.
She has to find the hand that holds her treat.
Can you help her find the treat?

Ella很会跳舞。

你是怎样跳舞的？

**Ella is a good dancer.
How do you dance?**

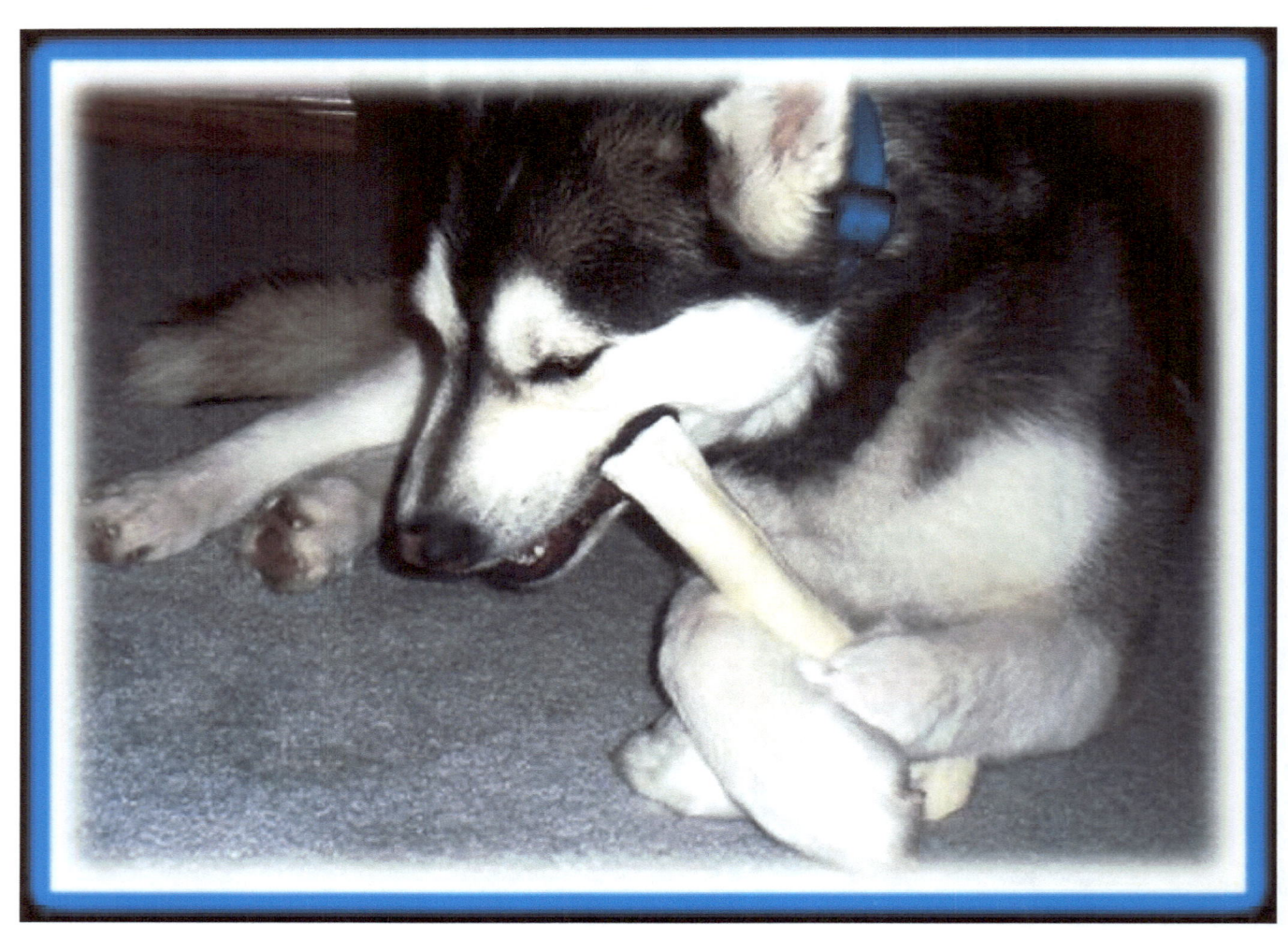

有时候Ella喜欢静下来嚼骨头...

Sometimes Ella just likes to rest and chew on her bone...

有时候她喜欢玩球。

and sometimes she plays with a ball.

Ella喜欢亲吻人们…

Ella likes to give kisses to people…

用她长长的舌头！

with her long tongue!

Ella也喜欢拥抱人们。

Ella likes to hug people too.

今天Ella将要乘车去兜风。

哦不！Ella没有系安全带！

Today Ella is going for a ride in the car.
Oh no! She is not wearing a seat belt!

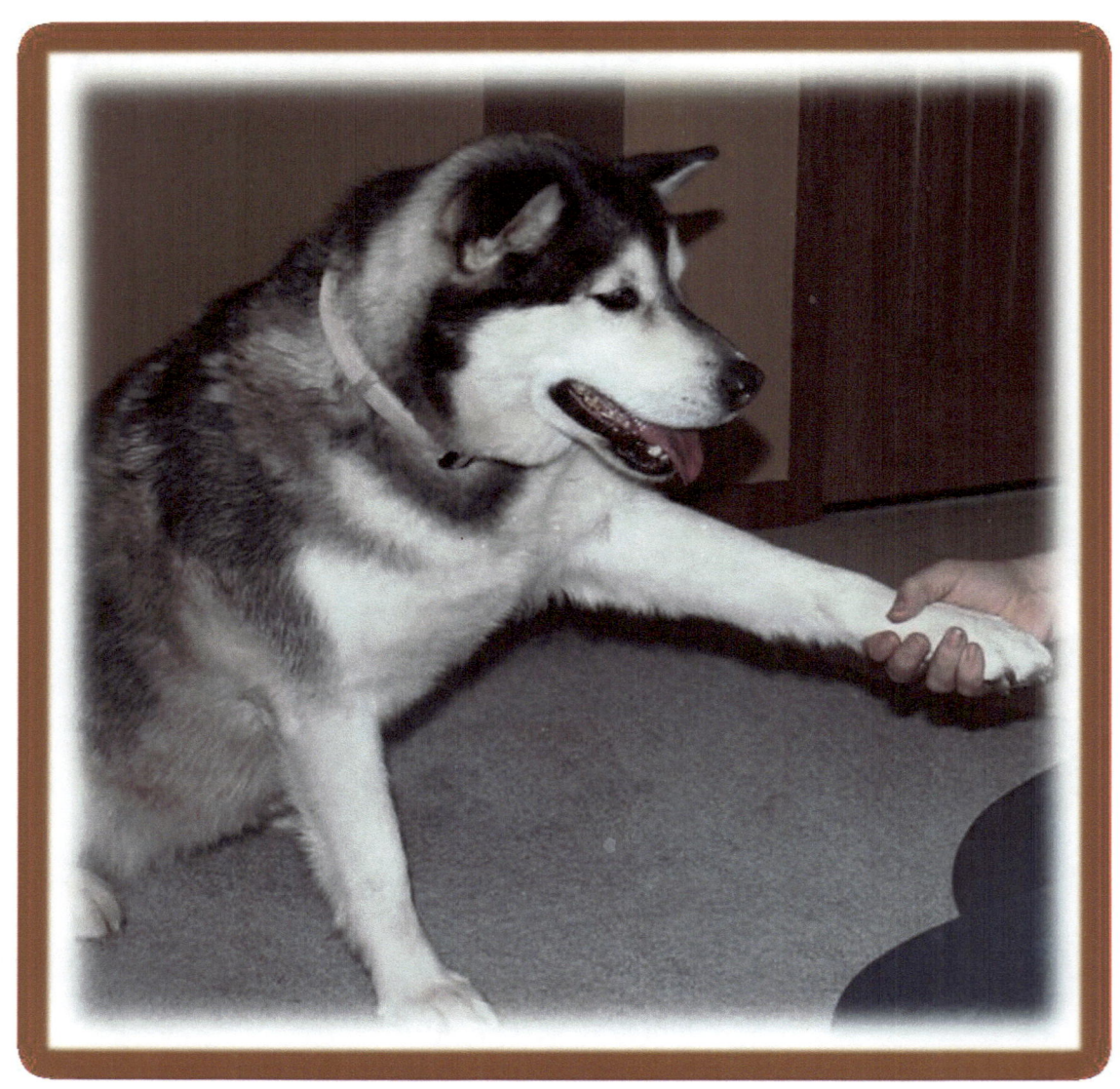

当Ella认识新朋友时，Ella会摇一摇她的爪子…

When she meets new people, Ella shakes with her paw…

然后当她激动的时候她会与人"击掌"。
and she gives a "*high five*" when she is excited.

你是摇一摇你的小爪子还是小手呢？

你知道怎样"击掌"吗？

Do you shake with a paw or with a hand?

Do you know how to give "*high fives*"?

今天对于Ella来说是非常繁忙的一天。

It has been a very busy day for Ella.

等等…她现在要去哪儿？

But wait...where is she going?

Ella在这里！她正朝窗外望去。

Ella正在思考着会让她明天忙碌起来的所有事情。

Here is Ella! She is looking out the window.

Ella is thinking about all of the things that will keep her busy tomorrow!

狗狗Ella

Ella the Doggy

Copyright © 2014 Jayne Flaagan Cover Design © 2014 Jayne Flaagan Pictures by Jayne Flaagan

版权 © 2014 Jayne Flaagan 封面设计© 2014 Jayne Flaagan图片来自Jayne Flaagan

No part of this publication may be reproduced in whole or in part, or stored in a retrieval system, or transmitted in any form or by any means, electronic, mechanical, photocopying, recording or otherwise, without written permission of the author.

该出版物的全部或部分不可转载或存储于检索系统，不能够以任何形式或手段如电子设备，机械，影印，录制或其它未经作者书面许可的形式传播。

如果你很喜欢"狗狗忙碌的一天"，我很感激你能够在亚马逊上留下评论。这还可以帮助其他更多的家庭来了解狗狗Ella。

此外，别忘了查看Ella的其他书籍。

If you enjoyed "Doggy's Busy Day," I would very much appreciate your leaving a review with Amazon. This will help other families learn about Ella the doggy too!

Also, don't forget to look for Ella's other books!

非常感谢！

Thank you!

Ella（狗狗）和Jayne（作者）

Ella (the doggy) and Jayne (the author)

www.ingramcontent.com/pod-product-compliance
Lightning Source LLC
Chambersburg PA
CBHW050757110526
44588CB00002B/34